334

PRAYERS FRC

C000203490

Catherine von Ruhland
specializing in art – particul
mental issues. She is the a
Glorious Food and lives in ....
West London.

Also by Catherine von Ruhland

Going Green (Marshall Pickering, 1991)
Glorious Food (Marshall Pickering, 1992)

PRAYERS
—— from the ——
EDGE

Meditations for Life's Tough Times

COMPILED AND EDITED BY

Catherine von Ruhland

TRIANGLE

First published in 1996

Triangle
Society for Promoting Christian Knowledge
Holy Trinity Church
Marylebone Road
London NW1 4DU

British Library Cataloguing-in-Publication Data
A catalogue record for this books is available from the British Library

ISBN 0-281-04846-0

Typeset by Wilmaset Ltd, Birkenhead, Wirral
Printed in Great Britain by BPC Paperbacks Ltd, Aylesbury

This book is dedicated with deep gratitude to all who work to the true benefit of the National Health Service and the people dependent on it, and in particular to the staff, past and present, of the Renal Unit of Guys Hospital, London.

Come to me, all you who are weary and burdened, and I will give you rest.
Take my yoke upon you and learn from me, for I am gentle and humble in heart, and you will find rest for your souls. For my yoke is easy and my burden is light.

Matt. 11. 28–9

Contents

INTRODUCTION

The people whose pieces are included here are those to whom I owe very many thanks. Although many of them are still facing life's trials, they had time for my correspondence and responded swiftly and courageously with prayers, poems, Bible verses, and moving anecdotes. What I'd originally envisaged as a straightforward collection of prayers has evolved into what I hope will prove to be a rich resource of a range of writing that reveals how God in his myriad ways has time and care for each one of us yesterday, today, forever.

That is something that I have tried to capture in the shape of this book, starting from a sense of hopelessness with Jesus' words on the cross, and moving onwards through the book to reveal the redemptive resurrection power and strength that God gives to those who trust in him. I pray that the prayers here will likewise touch you.

Catherine von Ruhland

Hope Lies Bleeding

Eloi, Eloi, lama sabachthani? . . . My God, my God, why have you forsaken me?

Mark 15. 34

THE SERENITY PRAYER

God, grant me the serenity to accept the things I cannot
   change,
The courage to change the things I can,
And the wisdom to know the difference.
Amen.

Reinhold Niebuhr (1892–1971), the distinguished American scholar
whose aim was to relate theology to the everyday world.

YOU'VE BEEN THERE, LORD

Fifteen months and nineteen days,
Then suddenly, all is gone
wrenched apart
torn away.
'Till death us do part' we said.
Who was to know?
Who could have imagined?
Why?
Why did God bring us together
under such unusual circumstances
– only to be shattered,
separated,
after such a brief time
forever in this life?
Why God? Why?

How can I complain?
How can I question
'why me?'
How can my self-centredness last
for more than a few moments
when I consider you,
and all you went through
– for me?

God is no stranger to death,
to pain, to suffering,
to separation from a loved one.

Lord Jesus, you've been there already,
You didn't shy away;
You didn't drift up to heaven.
But you suffered
the humility and degradation
the injustice and disgrace
the pain, the torment, the torture
the agony of mind and body.
You've been there already
– and you know.

Your death was not wasted
but served a purpose
the greatest purpose of all
– that of securing our salvation!

So I believe,
Charles' death cannot be wasted;
because to those who love you
all things work together for good.

Lesley Bilinda,
Edinburgh, 2 January 1995

'You've been there, Lord' was written on what would have been
Lesley Bilinda's second wedding anniversary. Her Rwandan
husband Charles was murdered in the country's civil war.

WE PRAY FOR THOSE WHO DO NOT KNOW YOU

We pray for those who do not know you,
for those who struggle with doubt,
for the lonely and those in despair,
for families under great stress,
for all who are homeless,
for all prisoners and those with responsibilities for them,
for those whose lives are being damaged by addiction,
for the many who are unemployed,
for young people as they look to the future,
for the elderly who may feel unwanted,
for those who are rich but are careless for others,
for all who praise you in word but not in life.

Lord, make your ways known to us all, open our eyes to see
    the needs of others and help us
to do your will, for Jesus' sake. Amen.

The Church Army

Dear Lord Jesus,
I don't know who I am,
I don't know what I am
I don't know where I am,
but please love me.

'This is the prayer Clive's late mother prayed whilst suffering from Alzheimer's disease,' remembers Ruth Calver, wife of the President of the Evangelical Alliance. 'She was in a very advanced stage. She was unable to communicate verbally. She had no idea of who she was and who we were. She basically mumbled and muttered away with the occasional recognizable word.

'I arrived at her home one morning to find her extremely distressed. The care assistant told me not to worry because they knew to cheer her up by telling my mother-in-law dirty jokes. Clive's mum, Flora Calver, was a Christian and had been in the Brethren most of her life; for her, dirty jokes were unheard of.

'I eventually managed to get her to her room. Physical mobility was by now severely restricted. I sat her on the bed and asked if she would like me to read some scriptural verses and then pray with her. Amazingly she said 'Yes'. After this, only the Lord could have prompted me to ask her if she would like to pray – by now a virtual impossibility. What happened was an incredible miracle.'

Lord,
I pray that we should have faith and trust in you my God,
even when we think there is no hope
because you are our true God
and you never let us down.

World Vision[1]

World Vision is an international Christian Third World development agency supporting such programmes as childcare among
Rwandan refugees, the distribution of relief supplies in Sudan,
reforestation in Ethiopia, and community work among the slum-
dwellers of Bangladesh's capital Dhaka. It was World Vision that
assisted broadcaster Michael Buerk in filming the 1984 footage of
famine in Ethiopia that moved viewers and inspired Bob Geldof's
Band Aid and Live Aid projects to raise millions of pounds for
Africa.

Lord Jesus
Help us to trust you
even when we are going through
the most trying times of our lives;
to know that you are there with us
and that your faithfulness is just.
Amen.

World Vision

The righteous cry out, and the Lord hears them;
he delivers them from all their troubles.
The Lord is close to the broken-hearted
and saves those who are crushed in spirit.

A righteous man may have many troubles,
but the Lord delivers him from them all;
he protects all his bones,
not one of them will be broken.

Ps. 34. 17–20

To you, O Lord, I called;
to the Lord I cried for mercy:
'What gain is there in my destruction,
in my going down into the pit?
Will the dust praise you?
Will it proclaim your faithfulness?
Hear, O Lord, and be merciful to me;
O Lord, be my help.'

You turned my wailing into dancing;
you removed my sackcloth and clothed me with joy,
that my heart may sing to you and not be silent.
O Lord my God, I will give you thanks for ever.

Ps. 30. 8–12

THE CRIPPLE AT THE GATE BEAUTIFUL
(Acts 3. 1–6)

I come to church
Clutching my begging bowl,
Two hand held
Head shame bent

  Have mercy, Lord,
  Have mercy, Lord,
  Have mercy, Lord,
   On me.

Thus crouched,
Tail cornered glimpse
Is all I see.
Hand occupied
I cannot reach
To touch his garment,
Even fleetingly.

The Gate is open,
But gravity
Self centred
Holds me down.
But, standing,
He commands my
Eyes to rise.

And then, and then,
Daring to look,
Straightness comes.
At last I see,
The Gate Beautiful
  It is he.

Jennifer Coleman

Jennifer Coleman is a full-time carer for her chronically ill husband. 'When this poem was written, in response to a sermon at an evening service, I was at a very low ebb, emotionally and physically, and was turned in on myself.'

PRAYER OF CONFESSION

Father eternal, giver of light and grace,
we have sinned against you
and against our neighbours,
in what we have thought,
in what we have said and done,
through ignorance, through weakness,
through our own deliberate fault.

We have wounded your love,
and marred your image in us.
We are sorry and ashamed,
and repent of all our sins.

For the sake of your Son Jesus Christ,
who died for us,
forgive us all that is past;
and lead us out from darkness
to walk as children of light.
Amen.

PRAYER OF HUMBLE ACCESS

Most merciful Lord,
your love compels us to come in.

Our hands were unclean,
our hearts were unprepared;
we were not fit
even to eat the crumbs from under your table.

But you, Lord, are the God of our salvation,
and share your bread with sinners.

So cleanse and feed us
with the precious body and blood of your Son,
that he may live in us and we in him;
and that we, with the whole company of Christ,
may sit and eat in your kingdom.
Amen.

The late Revd Simon Bailey was the Rector of Dinnington, South Yorkshire, and had AIDS. His 80-strong congregation rallied round to care for him in order that he could continue working, and his story featured in the national press and on BBC Television in *Everyman*. 'The Alternative Prayers of Confession and Humble Access have come to express for me some of the longing that I feel in the Eucharist.'

COLLECT FOR PURITY

Almighty God,
to whom all hearts are open,
all desires are known,
and from whom no secrets are hidden:
cleanse the thoughts of our hearts
by the inspiration of your Holy Spirit,
that we may perfectly love you,
and worthily magnify your holy name;
through Christ our Lord.
Amen.

'Actually my "first love", and often the prayer instinctively on my lips, is the Collect for Purity . . .' The Revd Simon Bailey.

Father,
Into your hands
I commit my spirit.

Luke 23. 46

THE BEATITUDES

Blessed are the poor in spirit,
for theirs is the kingdom of heaven.
Blessed are those who mourn,
for they will be comforted.
Blessed are the meek,
for they will inherit the earth.
Blessed are those who hunger and thirst for righteousness,
for they will be filled.
Blessed are the merciful,
for they will be shown mercy.
Blessed are the poor in heart,
for they will see God.
Blessed are the peacemakers,
for they will be called sons of God.
Blessed are those who are persecuted because of righteous-
    ness,
for theirs is the kingdom of heaven.

Matt. 5. 3–10

Abba, Father,
everthing is possible for you.
Take this cup from me.
Yet not what I will,
but what you will.

Mark 14. 36

Father in heaven,
I believe that you are and you live.
You have the power to give life to everyone and the power to take it away.
Now I ask you to take my life, Lord, because I cannot keep on suffering like this.
My body is covered with red nodules, and very painful.
Why must I have leprosy?
Lord, I am disappointed and desperate.
You have already taken away my parents,
and my family has chased me away because of this disease.
I want to die, because my life is useless.
But if you don't want me to die yet, I ask you to heal me, Lord.
Help me; my life or my death I surrender into your hands.

Father,
again I come to you.
This time I want to give you thanks,
because you have opened a way for me,
and I received clofazimine[2] free of charge.
Because I don't have money, this medicine is very valuable to me.
And I know that all this is from you.
Thank you Lord for your help.

Father,
before I was ill I never knew you.
I never knew that you loved me.
My life was far away from you, Lord.
Father,
forgive my sins.
Thank you.
Now I know the Lord has saved my soul.

My Lord,
I want to offer you something but I don't have anything.
I ask: use my life as your instrument.
I want to rejoice your heart.
Father,
hear my prayer.
In the name of the Lord Jesus I pray.
Amen.

Cured sufferer from Hansen's disease at Tangerang, Indonesia

Throughout history, people with the disease traditionally known as leprosy have suffered great stigma and been treated as outcasts. In the 1940s, the World Health Organisation gave up using the word 'leper', and in recent years, the disease has become known by the name of the Norwegian doctor who first identified the bacillus under the microscope.

O Lord, take me,
All that I am,
All that I have,
And break me,
If it be thy will,
To remake me
According to thy will,
That through me thy will
May be done.
Amen.

'This prayer is one we frequently recited during ballet school chapel services,' remembers Julie Sheldon. 'It is one that I probably didn't believe God would hear as I said it aged eleven, and certainly didn't believe God might answer it. I had no idea what the "breaking and remaking" might involve.

'That came in the form of dystonia, an incurable neurological illness. The effects were devastating. My body that I had carefully trained for fifteen years in order to be a ballet dancer, became totally out of control. Fierce muscle spasms distorted my limbs to the point that I was confined to a wheelchair and needed splints, neck collar and much medication. Used to being watched for my beautiful movements, it was utterly humiliating to be stared at because of the strange contortions into which my body now twisted and curled.

'The old school prayer came flooding back to mind. If this was the breaking of "all that I am and all that I have", surely the remaking would come soon? A friend was given a prophecy, a word from God, that he wrote down for me:

My child, I am well pleased with you. I delight in you and love you greatly. I think of you all the time. I have cried when you have cried, and I have suffered as you have suffered. Have faith and trust in me, for I am with you always. Put your hand in mine and walk with me along the path that I have prepared for you. Endure but for a short while, my little one, and you will share with me my crown of glory, and partake of the great and wonderful joys that I have prepared for you.

'I read and re-read this, hoping for its truth and fulfilment. After three years of severe and increasing disability, watching my husband and young daughters cope with a disabled wife and mother, the "enduring for a short while" felt like eternity. The "remaking" came at a critical time with a visit from Canon Jim Glennon who prayed by my hospital bed. He believed and prayed for my healing "without doubting in his heart" (Mark 11. 20–6). That prayer and visit was the beginning of total physical restoration, and the start of great and wonderful joys as mind and spirit were also broken and remade.'

The Long Wait

BITTER SWEET

Ah my dear angry Lord,
Since thou dost love, yet strike;
Cast down, yet help afford;
Sure I will do the like.

I will complain, yet praise;
I will bewail, approve;
And all my sour-sweet days
I will lament, and love.

George Herbert (1593–1633) was ordained a priest in 1630 and
worked for the rest of his life in the parish of Bemerton in
Wiltshire, near Salisbury.

He who dwells in the shelter of the Most High
will rest in the shadow of the Almighty.
I will say of the Lord, 'He is my refuge and my fortress,
my God, in whom I trust.'

Surely he will save you from the fowler's snare
and from the deadly pestilence.
He will cover you with his feathers,
and under his wings you will find refuge;
his faithfulness will be your shield and rampart.
You will not fear the terror of night,
nor the arrow that flies by day,
nor the pestilence that stalks in the darkness,
nor the plague that destroys at midday.
A thousand may fall at your side,
ten thousand at your right hand,
but it will not come near you.
You will only observe with your eyes
and see the punishment of the wicked.

If you make the Most High your dwelling –
even the Lord, who is my refuge –
then no harm will befall you,
no disaster will come near your tent.
For he will command his angels concerning you
to guard you in all your ways;
they will lift you up in their hands,
so that you will not strike your foot against a stone.
You will tread upon the lion and the cobra;
you will trample the great lion and the serpent.

'Because he loves me,' says the Lord, 'I will rescue him;
I will protect him, for he acknowledges my name.
He will call upon me, and I will answer him;
I will be with him in trouble,

I will deliver and honour him.
With long life will I satisfy him
and show him my salvation.'

Ps. 91

Those who trust in the Lord are like Mount Zion,
which cannot be shaken but endures for ever.
As the mountains surround Jerusalem,
so the Lord surrounds his people
both now and for evermore.

The sceptre of the wicked will not remain
over the land allotted to the righteous,
for then the righteous might use
their hands to do evil.

Do good, O Lord, to those who are good,
to those who are upright in heart.
But those who turn to crooked ways
the Lord will banish with the evildoers.

Peace be upon Israel.

Ps. 125

John and Jemima Munyaneza, who had acted like parents to
Lesley Bilinda during her years in Rwanda, witnessed the slaughter
of neighbours in their village at the height of the civil war: 'In
those terrible times God showed us the words of Psalm 91 and
Psalm 125, and we know that in all of this we are surrounded and
kept by his angels.'

Like millions of their compatriots, the Munyanezas sought
refuge in neighbouring Tanzania.

But now, this is what the Lord says –
he who created you, O Jacob,
he who formed you, O Israel:
'Fear not, for I have redeemed you;
I have called you by name; you are mine.
When you pass through the waters,
I will be with you;
and when you pass through the rivers,
they will not sweep over you.
When you walk through the fire,
you will not be burned;
the flames will not set you ablaze.
For I am the Lord, your God,
the Holy One of Israel, your Saviour.

Isa. 43. 1–3

'When I was separated from my family and was alone, I was so sad,'
reveals Louise Kambibi, friend and housegirl to Lesley Bilinda,
writing from a Tanzanian refugeee camp after fleeing the Rwandan
civil war. 'I cried a lot and thought I was nearly turning mad.
That's when I saw those words from Isaiah 43. When I'd read
them, I saw that God had rescued me and I sang. When God has
chosen you he helps you in everything.'

IF I EVER LOSE MY FAITH IN YOU

You could say I lost my faith in science and progress
You could say I lost my belief in the holy Church
You could say I lost my sense of direction
You could say all of this and worse but
If I ever lose my faith in you
There'd be nothing left for me to do

Some would say I was a lost man in a lost world
You could say I lost my faith in the people on TV
You could say I'd lost my belief in our politicians
They all seemed like game show hosts to me
If I ever lose my faith in you
There'd be nothing left for me to do

I could be lost inside their lies without a trace
But every time I close my eyes I see your face
I never saw no miracle of science
That didn't go from a blessing to a curse
I never saw no military solution
That didn't always end up as something worse but
Let me say this first
If I ever lose my faith in you
There'd be nothing left for me to do.

Sting, from the album *Ten Summoner's Tales*. Superficially a love
song about a woman, 'If I Ever Lose My Faith in You' can also be
interpreted as a prayer. Musician and songwriter Sting has shown
active concern for environmental and human rights issues through
support for rainforest campaigns and Amnesty International.

O JESUS, I HAVE PROMISED

O Jesus, I have promised
To serve thee to the end;
Be thou for ever near me,
My Master and my Friend:
I shall not fear the battle
If thou art by my side,
Nor wander from the pathway
If thou wilt be my guide.

O let me hear thee speaking
In accents clear and still,
Above the storms of passion,
The murmurs of self-will;
O speak to reassure me,
To hasten or control;
O speak, and make me listen,
Thou guardian of my soul.

O Jesus, thou has promised
To all who follow thee,
That where thou art in glory
There shall thy servant be;
And, Jesus, I have promised
To serve thee to the end:
O give me grace to follow,
My Master and my Friend.

O let me see thy foot-marks,
and in them plant mine own;
My hope to follow duly
Is in thy strength alone:
O guide me, call me, draw me,
Uphold me to the end;
And then in heaven receive me,
My Saviour and my Friend.

John Bode (1816–74) was Rector of Castle Camps, Cambridge-shire. He wrote this hymn for the confirmation of his two sons and one daughter in 1866.

THE BRETON FISHERMEN'S PRAYER

My boat is small
Your sea so vast
Dear Lord
protect me

'The Breton fishermen's prayer expresses in its brevity for me all the trust I need and hope when I'm faced with the vast ocean around and ahead of me.' The Revd Simon Bailey, who has AIDS.

THE LORD'S PRAYER

Our Father, who art in heaven,
Hallowed be thy name;
Thy kingdom come;
Thy will be done;
On earth as it is in heaven.
Give us this day our daily bread.
And forgive us our trespasses,
As we forgive those who trespass against us.
And lead us not into temptation;
But deliver us from evil.
For thine is the kingdom, the power and the glory,
For ever and ever.
Amen.

Gary McClure, a former prisoner on a life sentence and a lay member of the Order of St Francis, recalls a time of deep despair in his life when in the space of a few days he had lost his job as catering manager in a South African hotel, and his wife of three weeks had left. As a British citizen, he had to leave the country.

'I had lost everything. And God, or so I thought, was a million miles away. I decided to take my life, and prepared a noose on my ceiling trap door.

'I do not know what made me do it, for I had not prayed for years. But I knelt down to recite the Lord's Prayer. Halfway through it, there was a knock at the door. I opened it and there was a couple standing there who were related to my wife. They told me that they had had a message to collect me and that I wasn't to remain on my own. And when I asked where the message came from, they replied "From God".

'I went to put the rope away, but they told me that I didn't have to since they were well aware what I had intended to do with it. My legs became like jelly. I left with them, and three weeks later was back in the UK.'

Light at the End
of the Tunnel

CELEBRATION

Oh Lord, I thank you
For the cool and rainy days
In summer.
Oh Lord, I thank you
For the glimpse of the sun
In winter.
Oh Lord, I thank you for despair,
Which teaches me how good it is to hope.
Oh Lord, I thank you
For the trust I have in you.

And when the sun comes out again
I'll thank you for the golden glory of your world.
And when it starts to snow again
I'll thank you for the gleaming beauty of this land.
And when I know your joy again
I'll thank you for the peace within my heart.

Gillian McLeish, from Guildford: 'This poem was written when I was eighteen, just after I split up with my first serious boyfriend. I suffered from severe depression for several months, and only my faith in God prevented me from killing myself. Although I was not really a committed Christian at the time, I did believe in God, and I spent a lot of time reading Psalm 40 and crying out to God to give me the sense of trust in him which the first verses of the psalm express. *Celebration* came out of my mingled feelings of despair and knowledge that there was hope for the future.'

DEAR LORD AND FATHER OF MANKIND

Dear Lord and Father of mankind,
Forgive our foolish ways!
Re-clothe us in our rightful mind,
In purer lives thy service find,
In deeper reverence praise.

In simple trust like theirs who heard,
Beside the Syrian sea,
The gracious calling of the Lord,
Let us, like them, without a word
Rise up and follow thee.

O Sabbath rest by Galilee!
O calm of hills above,
Where Jesus knelt to share with thee
The silence of eternity,
Interpreted by love!

Drop thy still dews of quietness,
Till all our strivings cease;
Take from our souls the strain and stress,
And let our ordered lives confess
The beauty of thy peace.

Breathe through the heats of our desire
Thy coolness and thy balm;
Let sense be dumb,
Let flesh retire;
Speak through the earthquake, wind, and fire,
O still small voice of calm!

John Greenleaf Whittier (1807–92) was an American Quaker, farmer and journalist. From 1836 he was secretary of the American Anti-Slavery League.

The Lord is my shepherd, I shall lack nothing.
He makes me lie down in green pastures,
he leads me beside quiet waters,
he restores my soul.
He guides me in paths of righteousness
for his name's sake.
Even though I walk
through the valley of the shadow of death,
I will fear no evil,
for you are with me;
your rod and your staff,
they comfort me.

You prepare a table before me
in the presence of my enemies.
You anoint my head with oil;
my cup overflows.
Surely goodness and love will follow me
all the days of my life,
and I will dwell in the house of the Lord
for ever.

Ps. 23

Diagnosed as having cancer, Mel Blyth, a former employee of the
Christian Third World development agency, Tear Fund, suffered
months of severe anxiety and depression 'during which time, if I
prayed at all, it was usually a very simple cry to God for *help*! I did
cling very firmly to Psalm 23 when I was having an investigatory
scan at Hammersmith hospital as I thought I was going to have a
panic attack when they pushed me into the "tube"! (I *didn't* have
one and I *know* God helped me.)'

PAIN

Pain is hard to bear, Master,
even the dulled pain following sedation.
It stifles thought and smothers desire,
draining one of all but the longing to be free from its tyranny.
Help me to bear pain bravely, Lord,
without feeling sorry for myself
or envious of others less afflicted;
without venting my strained nerves on those around me.

Pain can teach me many lessons, Master.
It links me with suffering humanity all round the world,
levelling all classes, shades of colour and nationalities.
The groan of pain is the same in all languages,
it unites us all.
It is nature's warning that something is wrong,
and in that sense is invaluable,
but to be in constant pain, unalleviated,
is to be reduced in human potential.

I do not ask to escape pain, Lord, but I ask
to be able to bear my share of it where it is inevitable,
without feeling that you have forsaken me,
or ceased to care for me.
Let pain be your messenger to my heart.
Not a welcome one, certainly,
but one that can teach a lesson of endurance,
of compassion for others,
and of my great dependence upon you,
and your hourly help.

Flora Larsson is a retired Salvation Army officer. She is the author
of around 350 prayers on similar themes that she has written from
her imagination.

BED PATIENTS

My heart is at zero-point, Lord, and my spirits are flagging.
I feel desperately alone yet that is just what I am not.
I am one in a row of bed patients.
'This is your bed,' said the nurse kindly,
and I climbed into it with leaden feet.
My bed? For how long?
A frightened prospect of uncounted days loom before me.
I lie in total isolation of spirit,
not alone yet lonely,
with that desperate loneliness which seeps into every cell of
    the body,
and chills the mind.

From the fortress of my bed,
the only spot which is mine for the time being,
I survey the scene.
The business of the ward continues,
voices, laughter, footsteps, trolley-wheels passing,
all of them a curtain shutting me in upon myself.
Master, I cling to you now in wordless prayer.
Take away my fear, quiet my spirit,
let me burst out of this well of misery within
to find what is positive and good.

The patients on each side of me smile a greeting.
Shall I be as calm as they when I have settled in?
O help me, Lord! I trust in you.
You are with me here just as in my own home.
Let me believe it, even if I do not feel it.
Let me rest in your love,
even when I cannot frame a prayer.

Flora Larsson

UNDER OBSERVATION

Cold panic grips me, Master, and I shudder,
here between the sheets of this well-made bed,
too impersonal for my liking.
After a brief farewell my loved ones went,
leaving me in hospital 'for observation'.
The very words chill me . . .
I have a feeling of eyes watching me,
invisible eyes hidden in the ceiling,
stealthy eyes peering from under beds.
'Under observation' . . .
The doctors are kind and competent,
the nurses cheery and helpful,
the other patients sympathetic,
but I feel so alone, so helpless, so anxious
about the future.

I wipe away a silent tear.
You must forgive me for crying, Lord.
I don't usually give way like this.
Help me to be brave.
A quiet thought comes to me bringing courage, bringing
    comfort.
I'm under observation, under *your* observation, Master,
You know where I am, you know all about me;
Your loving glance rests upon me in compassion,
Your all-seeing eye spies out my distress.
You know what lies before me, ere even the doctors find out.
I'm not alone, I'm not abandoned,
I'm in your loving care.

Thank you, Master. My tears have dried
and I lift my heart to you in childlike confidence,
knowing that I am under your observation
and in your will.

Flora Larsson

'For I know the plans I have for you,' declares the Lord,
'plans to prosper you and not to harm you, plans to give
you hope and a future.'

Jer. 29. 11

Romanian teenager Adriana Dobre lost her legs when she fell
beneath a train in her home country. Members of Whaddon Way
Church, Bletchley, Milton Keynes have supported Adriana
through the medical treatment and schooling she has undergone
in the UK. Church administrator Margaret Cave recalls: 'I shared
with Adriana a text which has meant a great deal to my husband
Roy and me over the years. I pointed it out to her when the going
got tough and she felt we were just asking too much of her. I sat
down with her and looked back over the way the Lord had led us
each step of the way in her rehabilitation, providing the right help
at just the right time. Some passing comment of Adriana's when
we were in Romania last year gave me the impression that maybe
this verse has meant a lot to her too. Even after Adriana's
accident, when she seemed condemned to a lonely and useless life
as a disabled person in Romania, his plan to give her hope and a
future was beginning to unfold.'

SPEAK TO US OF CHILDREN

Your children are not your children
They are the sons and daughters of life's longing for itself.
They come through you but not from you,
And though they are with you, they belong not to you.
You may give them your love but not your thoughts
For they have their own thoughts.
You may house their bodies but not their souls,
For their souls dwell in the houses of tomorrow,
Which you cannot visit not even in your dreams.
You may strive to be like them, but seek not to make them
    like you.
For life goes not backward nor tarries with yesterday.
You are the bows from which your children as living arrows
    are sent forth.
The Archer sees the mark upon the path of the infinite,
and he bends it with his might that his arrows may go swift
    and far.
Let your bending in the Archer's hand be for gladness
For even as he loves the arrow that flies
so too does he love the bow that is stable.

Kahlil Gibran (1883–1931) was a Lebanese Christian poet, philospher and artist[3]

UNICEF worker Sean Devereaux, 28, was murdered in 1993 by a hired gunman in Somalia, for his outspokenness about the arms trade and the West's, including the British Government's, export of weaponry to the country's warlords.

Says his bereaved mother Maureen: 'I know that Sean's death in a strange way for me makes me see life with all its meaning. Even the flower in the garden is not my flower. I do not know how to create flowers. All I can do is nurture and care for them, just as we do our children. Sean gave me the words of *Speak to Us of Children*

47

the day before he died, and reading these profound words of Kahlil Gibran somehow helps me to accept, and see the greater meaning of life. And in some indefinable way Sean's presence remains with me even though he is not here.'

For you created my inmost being; you knit me together in my mother's womb.

Ps. 139. 13

Now a boistrous infant, Libby Smith was born prematurely and dangerously ill, and was to spend the first six weeks of her life in a special care unit. Her parents Alison and Julian recall the traumatic time: 'When Libby was first born and was very ill, we found Psalm 139 helped us both with the thought that God knows everything about us even when we are far from him.'

'Verse 13, indicating that God has known us from the very start, so he had created Libby too, gave me strength,' remembers Alison. 'I felt that if God knew Libby that well and created her that deliberately, then he would take care of her. That wasn't total assurance that she would live, but total assurance that he was in charge.

'It was a hard time in London when she was so close to death. I did say "Why me?" Everyone else was taking their babies home and having the thrill of being parents for the first time. A friend of mine said that God was allowing this to happen to us because he knew we could could cope, but I felt I wasn't coping at all.

'My parents certainly saw the comfort of the Lord keeping us going. My Dad, who isn't a Christian, wrote to us afterwards, saying how our faith had spoken to him, and how he had seen a strength in our marriage, and how material things didn't seem to matter to us. And that encouraged us a lot.'

O Blessed Lord Jesus,
Who suffered on the cross for me,
Bearing in your body not only my sins,
But the dark horror of the whole world's evil,
And with it all the griefs and the sorrows,
And the sicknesses of humankind,
Open now to me your great heart of compassion.

You, who once felt yourself to be forsaken of God,
Incline your ear to hear my cry,
My bitter cry of anguish.
A cry too deep for words.
Lord, I have so many questions.
There are so many things I do not understand.
But have mecy on me, I pray, O Lord,
And touch the chill gloom of my mind's darkness
With the flame of your love.

You are Love.
Enfold me then in that love, and make me know
That in your care I am safe forever:
That nothing in heaven or earth
Can separate me from that love –
Neither tribulation or distress;
Neither life, nor death;
Nor principalities or powers;
Neither things present, nor things to come –
Help the meaning of this great truth to sink into my soul.

Take, now, all my questions
And help me not to look for answers.
Take my pain, and make me willing
For you to transmute it into something beautiful for you.
Help me to rest in the shadow of your hand,
And to know that I and my loved ones
Are safe there, now, and throughout eternity.

In the name of the risen, conquering Saviour,
And because of his victory, I claim these things.
Amen.

Eileen Mitson, author and former columnist for *Woman Alive* magazine, remembers: 'As I stood by the bedside of my beautiful, ten-year-old daughter, and watched her slowly dying from leukaemia, I felt that the faith which had so marvellously sustained me throughout the long years of her illness was about to fail me. Somewhere in the painful darkness of my mind a small voice cried out: *"There's nobody there; there's nothing; nobody who cares."* The answer that seemed to come through to me was this: "You may let go of me, but I will never let go of you."

'After Frankie's death, I walked out into the garden and saw the apple tree ablaze with blossom. All around me the world was breaking out into new life. But my child was dead. Why had God given her to us, let us hold her and love her and watch her grow into loveliness for ten precious years, and then taken her away from us – slowly and painfully? I knew I was not the only person to have asked such a question. But at the time, this did nothing to ease the pain. Later, I was able to write this prayer.'

Dear Jesus,

It is a very important day for me because I had my transplant today. It went on all well but in the middle I got itching. The nurses had to stop it and they gave me an injection but it did not help a lot. Now also it is itching but I slept and prayed that Jesus will heal it before I got up. But I got up now and I am writing but the rashes are still there but they don't bother me too much because Jesus is saying "My grace is sufficient for you." Isn't it lovely that we have God's grace more than rashes so I trust Jesus will help me even as I come across more difficult circumstances. Help me to trust only in you and not in any medicine or doctor or anything. Help me to have a strong faith in you. I love you, Jesus. You are just great. You have been my everything, a refuge, my strength, my salvation and you have been a greatest father to me. I love you, Lord you are just too great. The transplant went on well and Thank you Jesus.

Love,

Sweety Peter

Twelve-year-old Sweety wrote the above diary entry to her 'best friend' Jesus on the day of her bone marrow transplant at the Medical College Hospital, Vellore, South India. Sadly, the drugs she needed to prevent rejection of her sister's bone marrow probably led to the severe liver complications that were to cause her death a month later. Betty Baker, with whom Sweety stayed while under medical observation in Oxford, reports on her visit to Sweety's bereaved family: 'We found them deeply grieving for a beloved child, but also rejoicing in the witness that Sweety had been during her short time on earth. It was very moving to be taken to the spot in the assembly hall of Sweety's school where she had gathered a little group of Hindu girls at break every day for a prayer time, as a result of which several came to know her Lord too. Moving too to hear the tape that she and her donor sister (the only person allowed into the isolation ward) had made of praise and songs and, refreshingly, outbursts of giggles, during the chemotherapy time when the beautiful blue-black hair which was her pride and joy was falling out in handfuls. As we wept together on the roof in the comparative cool of the Indian night, it was borne in upon us all that Sweety had in her twelve years done more for her beloved Jesus than most of us in three, four or five times that number, and we were both glad and ashamed.'

Have I not commanded you? Be strong and courageous.
Do not be terrified; do not be discouraged, for the Lord
your God will be with you wherever you go.

Josh. 1. 9

Charles Bester was only eighteen when he was sentenced to six
years' imprisonment in December 1988 for his refusal to serve in
the South African Defence Force. 'At the end of the first day of my
imprisonment I felt so bashed, and thought "Is this really right?"
However, that night I just lay on my bed, prayed and read my
Bible, and was drawn to this verse.' Charles was subsequently
released after twenty months' imprisonment for conscientious
objection. On his release in 1990 he said: 'I was told about people's
prayers for me. I really am very grateful for everyone's prayers.
Even when I was at my lowest I knew that people were behind me
and this gave me real encouragement. I'm still convinced that it is
the power of prayer which has been changing our land.'

For our struggle is not against flesh and blood, but against the rulers, against the authorities, against the powers of this dark world and against the spiritual forces of evil in the heavenly realms.

Eph. 6. 12

Nearing the end of a prison sentence, Eddie Murison had been tempted to smuggle drugs into gaol when on a day out, 'but though it was my idea in the first place, I could not go through with it, because I knew it would be sinning against God.' However, other men were involved and were threatening Eddie with knives if he didn't comply. His fear for his life drove him to consider retaliating likewise, but as a Christian he believed he shouldn't. 'It was pulling me apart inside,' he recalls. He chose to put his life in God's hands.

'God drew me to Ephesians 6. 12. After reading this I began to understand that my prayer should not be against people.' The next day Eddie, who had kept his cell door closed to protect himself, felt free to leave it open, 'not only that, but I went over to one of the men, took the knife from him, and told him that God did not want him to use it on me.

'The three men ended up in my cell and I was able to tell them about the love of Jesus in my own life. The fear had gone, and the men were to return, wanting to know more about my God.'

This is what your Sovereign Lord says,
your God, who defends his people:
'See, I have taken out of your hand
the cup that made you stagger; from that cup, the goblet of
    my wrath,
you will never drink again.'

Released from prison, Eddie Murison found himself prey to great temptation, and within months began drinking heavily. 'God went out the window. I didn't feel good about what I was doing and was getting into fights too because of the drink.' He ended up at a rehabilitation centre for alcoholics and during his stay attended a Christian conference which included a service in which people were asked to go to the front if they wanted God's help to overcome any problem.

'I felt I had to respond,' remembers Eddie, 'but I couldn't go forward. I said to God, "Lord, I need help for my drinking, but I'm not going forward for it." ' Yet once back at the rehab centre Eddie's mind remained on God. 'Once in my room I took out my Bible and it seemed to fall open at Isaiah 51. 22. The words leapt out at me. Something spoke to me deep down as I read them. I knew I was healed from drink, and have never had a drink since – that's over five years now.

'God was giving me freedom from things within me, so I've been set free from a different prison,' Eddie concludes. 'God's word is the truth, and the truth will set you free.'

FOOTPRINTS

One night a man had a dream. He dreamed he was walking
along the beach with the Lord.

Across the sky flashed scenes from his life. For each scene,
he noticed two sets of footprints in the sand; one
belonging to him, and the other to the Lord.

When the last scene of his life flashed before him, he looked
back at the footprints in the sand. He noticed that many
times along the path of his life there was only one set of
footprints. He also noticed that it happened at the very
lowest and saddest times in his life.

This really bothered him and he questioned the Lord about
it. 'Lord you said that once I decided to follow you, you'd
walk with me all the way. But I have noticed that during
the most troublesome times in my life, there is only one
set of footprints. I don't understand why when I needed
you most you would leave me.'

The Lord replied, 'My precious, precious child, I love you
and I would never leave you.

During your times of trial and suffering, when you saw only
one set of footprints, it was then that I carried you.'

Margaret Fishback Powers

A medical blunder in a routine operation in 1986 left Pat Joyce,
then 48, a victim of LIS: locked-in syndrome. Almost totally
immobilized, his only method of communication is via the raising
of his eyes to indicate 'yes', dropping them to say 'no'. Messages
are laboriously spelt out letter by letter and transcribed by
members of his loving family. When Pat is feeling low, *Footprints*,
a copy of which hangs above his hospital bed, gives him peace and
strength. 'I know that one day God will cure me. I put my trust in
God,' he says.

IMAGE: ST SEBASTIAN

O St Sebastian,
eyes raised,
prayer hands tied,
straining with all your might heavenward
to avoid the arrows' path.

Help me to look likewise
toward God,
so the slings and arrows
of hurts sent me
graze sparingly
and leave only
surface wounds.

Catherine von Ruhland, 24 February 1995

Based on a 'mind picture' given during prayer about handing to
God past grievances, and on the second day of news reports of
'shy, sensitive' actor Stephen Fry's walkabout across Europe
caused by stress over bad reviews for his appearance in the West
End play *Cell Mates*.

Lord,
There are two frustrations to my disability.
First the physical limitations,
but secondly the way in which people's attitudes to those
  limitations
poison their relationships with me.
Please help me to forgive them.

It feels painful that so many people now see me in terms of
  what I can't do,
or what I do differently,
rather than as the person I am.

Being inside this crippled body feels like being on the inside
  of a two-way mirror,
able to look out and see the 'normal' people,
but without their awareness that I am on the other side.

When they look at me and into the mirror they see not me,
but a reflection of themselves in my situation.
It is as if they have accidently walked into a hall of mirrors
at a fun-fair and been suddenly shocked by a grotesquely
  distorted
image of themselves,
their plans, their hopes . . . their futures.

This instinct is clear in their faces when they meet me,
or look at me from across the street or park.
If they don't look away and are forced to come nearer,
the more obvious this instinctive fear of me becomes.
Because it *is* fear they are feeling.
They are afraid of the same thing happening to them,
and those who do get closer
are afraid of my emotions about my disability.

So Lord,
please help me to forgive the way they react to me
because I find it so difficult.
And, Lord,
please forgive me too,
because before I became disabled,
I know that I reacted in the same way.
Amen.

As a healthy and fit twenty-eight year-old Peter Lockwood suffered a massive stroke completely without warning while flying alone to the USA on business. It was caused by a cerebral haemorrhage from a weakness in an artery which was probably congenital, and he is now confined to a wheelchair.

FORGIVENESS

O Lord, remember not only the men and women of
  goodwill,
but also those of ill will.

Do not remember all the suffering they have inflicted on us;
remember the fruits we bear, thanks to this suffering –
our comradeship,
our loyalty,
our humility,
courage,
generosity,
the greatness of heart which has grown out of all this.
And when they come to judgement,
let all the fruits that we have borne be their forgiveness.

A prayer found on a scrap of paper beside the body of a Jewish
woman who died at Ravensbruck concentration camp during the
Second World War.

No-one is useless in this world who lightens the burden of it for someone else.

Charles Dickens (1812–70)

'I came upon this quotation not long after being dismissed from my job,' recalls journalist Elizabeth Filleul. 'I was depressed and angry and felt worthless, useless and a failure. I even believed that the world would be a better place without me in it.

'Dickens' words reminded me of my parents, whose lives were hampered by illness, and who always looked forward to my visits home. And of my fiancé in Australia who thought I was worth coming 12,000 miles to marry. For the first time, I realized that an hour spent visiting my grandmother was more satisfying and important to her than anything I'd achieved in my career had ever been to me.

'Although my depression didn't lift for five months, I continually reminded myself of those words. Now, as I look ahead to a new life in Australia, I believe the whole episode changed my life and my priorities for the better. And I'm grateful to God for that.'

I will repay you for the years the locusts have eaten –
the great locust and the young locust,
the other locusts and the locust swarm –
my great army that I sent among you.

Joel 2. 25

'Why don't you do something?' Carol Carthy would demand of God as she watched her husband Paul slipping deeper into heroin addiction. 'But it didn't work. I wasn't really seeking God's answer to the problem. I knew exactly how I wanted him to deal with it. But God had a better idea.' With their eighteen-month marriage under great strain, Paul enrolled in Teen Challenge, a Christian rehabilitation centre in Wales, and after a year's treatment that meant separation from Carol, he overcame his addiction.

'God's promise to me throughout all of this was Joel 2. 25. He is repaying us now. He has given us a beautiful cottage in the Welsh countryside. I am working full-time and Paul has just launched his own business. God has rebuilt the trust in our marriage and we have already been able to help others going through similar situations.

'Things are by no means easy. We are completely different people from when we were married. But we are still trusting in God for our future. He has brought us this far. Who knows what the future holds with God at the centre of our life?'

I have come that they may have life, and have it to the full.

John 10. 10

'My immediate reaction to being told I was HIV positive was to ask myself the question, "Why shouldn't it happen to me?" ' says the Revd Joe Humble, who at the time was a Mission to Seamen chaplain in Buenos Aires. 'I had lived long enough to know that the world is full of disasters. Why should I be spared?

'And one of the Lord's parables which has always struck a chord with me, is about the two men who each built a house. One built on the sand, so when the storm came it was washed away. The other built on rock, and when the storm came the house stood. The rock of course stands for the words of Jesus (Matt. 7. 24–7). I have tried to listen to the words of Jesus and to build my life upon them. So when the storm came into my life I was not so surprised, and the house of my life has so far withstood the storm.

'The other saying of Jesus which sticks continually in my mind is the statement of his aim in life, John 10.10. So I have felt it almost a duty to do all I can to be alive.

'On the other hand my prayer has always been that I should have courage to face whatever comes my way.'

O Lord our God,
from whom neither life nor death
can separate us
from those who trust in your love,
and whose love holds in its embrace
your children in this world
and in the next,
so unite us to yourself,
that in fellowship with you
we may be always united
to our loved ones
whether here or there:
give us courage, constancy and hope;
through him who died and was buried
and rose again for us,
Jesus Christ our Lord.

William Temple (1881–1944), Archbishop of Canterbury, wrote
this for his wife at the time of the death of her mother.

DON'T BE SAD. BE THANKFUL FOR WHAT WE HAVE MEANT TO EACH OTHER

Thank you, Jesus,
for a mother's unfailing love,
for her unstinting devotion and steadfastness,
for her wisdom and support,
for always 'being there' in times of happiness and of stress.
And grant that, at the end,
she shall be given eternal rest in thy kingdom
after a lifetime of service to her family.

Diana Wiseman

Remembering the death of her mother, Diana writes: 'The arms which embraced me on the day I was born, which comforted me through the hurts of childhood, and of adulthood, which lovingly held my own children, lay still, in peaceful death.

'I gazed down at her beloved face, my brain not registering the significance of the moment, that I should never see her again. Later, sleepless, my mind overactive, I wondered and wondered, where was she – the vital, sparkling, wise, dependable rock, my mother? Was she near me, by my side, unseen, or had she moved away – already on 'that other shore'?

'I have no doubt that her unwavering faith, her unquestioning belief in the resurrection, ensures her a place in the eternal kingdom and that, with God's grace and in his time, we shall be reunited: the separation, even if long years in earthly measure, less than an eye's blink in eternity.'

May he be with God.
May he be with the living God.
May he be with the immortal God.
May he be in God's hands.
May he be where the great name of God is.
May he be where God's greatness is.
May he be with the living God
now and on the day of judgement.
Live in God, live in eternal delight.

Anon

Redemption Song

If I should die and leave you here awhile,
Be not like others sore, undone, who keep
Long vigils by the silent dust and weep.
For my sake turn again to life and smile,
Nerving thy heart and trembling hand to do
Something to comfort other hearts than thine,
Complete these dear unfinished tasks of mine,
And I, perchance may therein comfort you.

On the death of Labour Party leader John Smith in May 1994, his widow Elizabeth recalls: 'This poem was sent to me after my husband died, with a simple dedication which I found incredibly moving:

To: Mrs John Smith
From: An Edinburgh widow hoping it might comfort and
    sustain you.

'I read it over and over and it gave me great strength. I so much wanted to tell the anonymous lady how much it meant to me.'

DEATH IS NOTHING AT ALL

Death is nothing at all. I have only slipped away into the next room.

I am I, and you are you. Whatever we were to each other, that we still are. Call me by my old familiar name, speak to me in the easy way which you always used. Put no difference in your tone, wear no forced air of solemnity or sorrow.

Laugh as we always laughed at little jokes we enjoyed together.

Play, smile, think of me, pray for me.

Let my name be ever the household word that it always was, let it be spoken without effort, without the trace of a shadow on it. Life means all that it ever meant.

It is the same as it ever was;

there is unbroken continuity.

Why should I be out of mind because I am out of sight?

I am waiting for you, for an interval, somewhere very near, just round the corner.

All is well.

Henry Scott Holland (1847–1918), Canon of St Paul's Cathedral

Woolworth's trainee manager John Penfold, 21, was stabbed to death in November 1994 while on counter duty at the company's Teddington branch. 'The piece by Henry Scott Holland we have found very comforting,' reflect his bereaved parents, Madeline and Michael Penfold.

Grant unto us O Lord,
the royalty of inward happiness
and the serenity which comes from living close to thee.
Daily renew in us the sense of joy
and let thy eternal spirit
dwell in our souls and bodies,
filling every corner of our hearts with light and gladness;
so that, bearing about with us
the infection of a good courage,
we may be diffusers of life,
and meet all that comes, of good or ill,
even death itself,
with gallant and high hearted happiness:
giving thee thanks always for all things.
Amen.

Prayer for the Annual Service of the Distinguished Order of St Michael and St George for Service to the Crown.

I know not where his islands lift their
fronded palms in air:
I only know I cannot drift
beyond his love and care.

John Greenleaf Whittier (1807–92)

The late Senator Gordon Wilson's daughter Marie was killed on Remembrance Sunday 1987 when a bomb went off at the cenotaph in Enniskillen, Northern Ireland. Her father's words, which emerged out of obvious deep anguish, stirred the hearts of all who heard the news reports: 'I have lost my daughter, but I bear no ill will, I bear no grudge . . . Dirty sort of talk is not going to bring her back to life . . . I don't have an answer . . . But I know there has to be a plan. If I didn't think that, I would commit suicide . . . It's part of a greater plan, and God is good . . . And we shall meet again.'[4]

In late 1994, Senator Wilson and his wife Joan were again to experience the loss of a child when their son Peter, Marie's older brother, was killed. The Senator said that the words that helped him most were those from John Greenleaf Whittier's hymn 'All as God wills'.

But we have this treasure in jars of clay to show that this all-surpassing power is from God and not from us. We are hard pressed on every side, but not crushed; perplexed, but not in despair; persecuted, but not abandoned; struck down, but not destroyed. We always carry around in our body the death of Jesus, so that the life of Jesus may also be revealed in our body. For we who are alive are always being given over to death for Jesus' sake, so that his life may be revealed in our mortal body. So then, death is at work in us, but life is at work in you (. . .)

Therefore we do not lose heart. Though outwardly we are wasting away, yet inwardly we are being renewed day by day. For our light and momentary troubles are achieving for us an eternal glory that far outweighs them all. So we fix our eyes not on what is seen, but on what is unseen. For what is seen is temporary, but what is unseen is eternal.

2 Cor. 4. 7–12, 16–18

Entertainer, musician, record-breaking tap dancer, and television presenter Roy Castle's Christian faith sustained him during his eventually unsuccessful fight against lung cancer. 'This is one Bible chapter that Roy found great comfort in, his favoured version being found in the Living Bible,' says his widow Fiona.

Dear Heavenly Father,
I am praying with all my heart for my suffering to be cured.
I have been in The Leprosy Mission's Jesus Hospital for
   three years with skin cancer,
and have had leprosy since a child.
In this hospital I have come to know you as my Saviour
and realized your love through the staff's loving care.
I have been given real peace in my heart by your words.
I have neither hands nor feet
but my honest heart is running into your kingdom.
I pray that your blessing may be upon me to get out of this
   bed.
May you also bless TLM members throughout the world.
I pray in Jesus' name.
Amen.

Su Yung Kim, an in-patient at The Leprosy Mission's Jesus Hospital,
Taegu, Korea

My God, I pray that I may so know you and love you that I
    may rejoice in you
And if I may not do so fully in this life, let me go steadily on
to the day when I come to that fullness.
Let the knowledge of you increase in me here,
and there let it come to its fullness.
Let your love grow in me here,
and there let it be fulfilled,
so that here my joy may be in a great hope,
and there in full reality.

Anselm

Paul Stephenson is overseeing community services on behalf of
Tear Fund in Benaco refugee camp in Tanzania on the border with
Rwanda.

THE VEILED SITTER
(To Lionel Miskin)

Uncanny though not quite dark,
This rigid hour in which I sit
Marooned and fog-bound on the familiar chair.
Outside the cottage the rain and grit
Push mud to the lanes, and I am sealed
For a distant gallery's glare.
In the world of culture, elegance,
My trapped and truant mood should yield
Its fire on canvas. When the stranger's glance
Unfolds the artist's idiom, seeks the stark
Truth of my face, will the flame break through?

I send clue after clue
Against the fog-belt: a sparkle, a flash
Embeds itself where a thought should dash,
Spinning to blaze for the painter's eye.
But the signals die
Within the binding cloud: only the lips may show
By a sultry pucker, a softened rift,
How strange and rare is the sitter's gift
You would mediate and bestow.
The snaky mist
Has tunnelled down from a past so grim,
A fate so drab, a painter could limn
With Hogarth-smirch, Picasso-twist,
Yet not belie the pervert brow,
The humped will in the twilight. And what now?
You paint a man reborn through creed.

Pile on flamboyant colour: show my soul
Retrieved from the dead grey mask!
Bring Van Gogh riot to the task:
No wistful half-tones or granite glooms
Transmit the winged control.

Its bold rough bubbly light you need
To catch my spirit, trace the swerve
Away from the ego's fumes
And the tense blackened nerve.
The faithful lines will glow
With the convert's passion: you'll create
A hint of something shattered, and that's my fate.[5]

Jack Clemo (1916–94), Cornish poet and novelist

'*The Veiled Sitter* has always moved me deeply,' writes Jack Clemo's widow Ruth. 'It is one of his early poems which in spite of his double handicap of blindness and deafness is so full of buoyancy and life! Jack was sitting having his portrait painted outside the Goonamarris cottage in Cornwall. He wanted to make sure the painter captured on canvas his real self: "a man reborn through creed".'

O God in Jesus Christ you fell,
for love, into the dark earth
and died:
give us grace to wait in patient
hope and love for the rich harvest
you have promised, that will
blossom in our hearts with abundant
life and love for all the world:
through Jesus Christ we pray
who is the promise of your love
restored, renewed and multiplied.
Amen.

The Revd Simon Bailey

'I wrote this prayer for Good Friday using the picture of the seed that dies from John 12. I've used it also at funerals and it tries to find words, for me, to speak about my own dying.'

GRACE

O Lord:

In a world where many are lonely;
We thank you for our friendships.

In a world where many are captive;
We thank you for our freedom.

In a world where many are hungry:
We thank you for your provision.

We pray that you will:
Enlarge our sympathy,
Deepen our compassion,
And give us grateful hearts.

In Christ's name.
Amen.

Written by Terry Waite, who was the Archbishop of Canterbury's special envoy negotiating for the release of British hostages in Lebanon until 1987 when he himself was captured and held in Beirut for nearly five years.

WHEN I SURVEY THE WONDROUS CROSS

When I survey the wondrous cross
On which the Prince of Glory died,
My richest gain I count but loss
And pour contempt on all my pride.

See from his head, his hands, his feet
Sorrow and love flow mingled down,
Did e'er such love and sorrow meet
Or thorns compose so rich a crown?

Were the whole realm of nature mine
That were an offering far too small,
Love so amazing, so divine
Demands my soul, my life, my all.

Isaac Watts (1674–1748) was ordained as an independent minister in 1702. He was also an author and writer of some of the best-loved hymns in the English language.

Send me out
in the power of your spirit
to live and work
to your praise and glory.

Adapted from The Order for Holy Communion Rite A in the
Alternative Service Book, 1980.

Notes

1 *Lord, Make Me an Instrument*, World Vision, 1991.
2 Clofazimine: an anti-inflammatory agent that in higher doses kills the leprosy bacillus, and is now used internationally in the prescribed two-year course of multi-drug treatment to cure people of Hansen's disease.
3 Kahlil Gibran, 'Speak to Us of Children' in *The Prophet* (1926), Penguin, 1992, pp. 22–25.
4 Gordon Wilson, *Marie*, Marshall Pickering, 1990, p. xiv.
5 'Fate' here means the unredeemed ego.

Acknowledgements

Every effort has been made to trace the copyright holders of material quoted in this book. Information on any omission should be sent to the publishers who will make full acknowledgements in future editions.

All Bible references are from the *New International Version*, © 1973, 1978, 1984 by the International Bible Society. Published by Hodder & Stoughton.

Ordered by title or first line:

Alternative Confession. *The Alternative Service Book 1980*, © The Central Board of Finance of the Church of England, p. 166.

Alternative Prayer of Humble Access. *The Alternative Service Book 1980*. © The Central Board of Finance of the Church of England, p. 170.

Bed Patients. © Flora Larsson.

Celebration. © Gillian McLeish.

Collect for Purity. *The Alternative Service Book 1980*, © The Central Board of Finance of the Church of England, p. 119.

Collect in Times of Trouble. *The Alternative Service Book 1980*. © The Central Board of Finance of the Church of England, pp. 914 and 915.

Cripple at the Gate Beautiful, The. © Jennifer Coleman, 1995.

Dear God, Our Loving Father. ASK 1994, The Leprosy Mission, p. 8.

Dear Heavenly Father, I Am Praying With All My Heart. ASK 1995, The Leprosy Mission, p. 16.

Dear Jesus, It Was A Very Important Day. In 'Sweety Peter: A Brief Life' by Betty Baker, *Christian Impact Newsletter*, no. 8, Summer 1994, p. 6.

Dear Lord and Father of Mankind. *New English Hymnal*. Compilation by permission of The Canterbury Press, Norwich, pp. 359–360.

Don't Be Sad. Be Thankful For What We Meant To Each Other. © Diana Wiseman, 1995.

Father In Heaven, I Believe That You Are. ASK 1995, The Leprosy Mission, p. 7.

Forgiveness. *Prayers for Today's World*, © 1972, Dick Williams, Kingsway Publications.

Grace. © Terry Waite, 1995.

Grant Unto Us, O Lord. Margaret Pawley, ed., *Praying for People*, SPCK, 1992, p. 131.

If I Ever Lose My Faith In You. © Bugle Songs Ltd.

Living With Mistakes. © Flora Larsson.

Lord, There Are Two Frustrations. © Peter Lockwood, 1993.

May He Be With God. Margaret Pawley, ed., *Praying for People*, SPCK, 1992, p. 104.

My Lord And My King. *ASK 1993*, The Leprosy Mission, p. 36.

O Blessed Lord Jesus. © Eileen Mitson.

O Jesus I Have Promised. *New English Hymnal*. Compilation by permission of The Canterbury Press, Norwich, pp. 418–419.

O Lord Our God From Whom Neither Life Nor Death Can Separate Us. Margaret Pawley, ed., *Praying for People*, SPCK, 1992, p. 105.

O My Loving Heavenly Father. *ASK 1994*, The Leprosy Mission, p. 20.

Pain. © Flora Larsson.

Under Observation. © Flora Larsson.

Veiled Sitter, The. © Ruth Clemo.

We Pray For Those Who Do Not Know You. Church Army.

You've Been There Lord. © Lesley Bilinda, 1995.

Triangle Books
can be obtained from all good bookshops.
In case of difficulty, or for a complete list of our books, contact:
SPCK Mail Order
36 Steep Hill
Lincoln
LN2 1LU
(tel: 01522 527486)